4

NATASHA JESHANI

THE HR INSIDER — HOW TO LAND YOUR DREAM JOB AND KEEP IT

ISBN-13: 978-1717475565

ISBN-10: 1717475566

Copyright © 2018 Natasha Jeshani

All rights reserved under International and Pan-American Copyright Conventions.

Manufactured in the United States of America

Editor **ELIZABETH THE**

Cover Design **ANGELA STEVENS**

Book Design **JAZMIN WELCH**

Publishing Support **THE SELF PUBLISHING AGENCY**

THE HR
INSIDER

HOW TO LAND YOUR
DREAM JOB, AND KEEP IT

NATASHA JESHANI

Improve your chances of finding,
landing and keeping your dream job!

BONUS: intentions worksheets and
thought-provoking questionnaires
to get you started today!

EDITION
01

INTRO TO MY INTRO

I owe my success in large part to the ones that pushed me, mentored me and taught me; to the ones that picked me up and dusted me off when I felt like giving up.

Throughout this book, I share invaluable quotes from these incredible professionals and thank them for allowing me to get to where I am today.

No one does it alone, and if you think you did it alone, you are not nearly as successful as you could be.

I am truly inspired by the ones that shaped me.

Everyone has their own version of the dream job. For me, it was leaving my nine-to-five (or nine-to-nine) and starting a consulting firm on my own.

For many of my clients, it's about being able to wake up excited to go to work, get there and feel valued and fulfilled, and go home feeling respected and appreciated.

This book is your guide to taking your job search and career into your own hands and learning how to effectively control the various stages of the job search process.

Get your pen and highlighter ready, it's time to get to work!

INTRO

The fact that you've picked up this book, whether it was to buy and read from front to back, to scan the back of the book for a quick tip, or just out of curiosity to see if this is for you; it means that you are already one step closer to your dream job.

Admittedly, there are many ways to land a great job. Although it is important to understand the process involved so that you can be at the top of your game, the sheer desire to land the job and the belief that it's even remotely possible is the right way of thinking.

Throughout the book, you will notice a series of questions being asked. It's important to stop and answer these questions and give yourself some time to reflect on what you are reading and what your intentions are with the information you've just read.

Good luck with your job search – even though by the end of the book, you'll come to see that luck has nothing to do with it!

TABLE OF CONTENTS

1 BEFORE YOU START   9

2 THE RESUME part 1   17

3 THE RESUME part 2   25

4 THE COVER LETTER   31

5 SOCIAL MEDIA   39

6 NETWORKING   47

7 THE PHONE SCREEN   53

8 THE INTERVIEW   59

9 THE INTERVIEWER   67

10 AFTER THE INTERVIEW   75

11 THE OFFER   81

12 THE CHECK IN   87

13 THE JOB   93

CHECKLISTS & RESOURCES   101

"

IF YOU'RE UNHAPPY
IN YOUR JOB
RE-EVALUATE
YOUR GOALS
RE-INVEST
IN YOURSELF
RE-IGNITE
YOUR PASSION.

NATASHA JESHANI

BEFORE YOU START

You can increase your chances of landing your dream job by increasing the effectiveness of your job search.

Let's look at what that entails:

1 FOCUS ON THE FUTURE

Don't worry about that last degree, that last job, or that last boss. Focus on what you want moving forward. Know what you are looking for, and then start your path toward achieving that.

2 DON'T LET THE NEGATIVITY IN

We all have things to deal with. Push them aside when you are working on your job search. There is power in confidence, in positive thinking and in bouncing back. Don't let the current negativity affect the future good.

3 TAKE CARE OF YOURSELF

First impressions are important, you can't make a positive first impression if you aren't taking care of yourself. Losing a job or being unhappy in your current role doesn't give you an excuse to let yourself go.

Self-care is such an important part of controlling what you **can** control. Some examples of self care are:

- taking pride in how you present yourself professionally
- spending time on your personal and professional development
- taking time out of your day to do something because you want to, not because you have to.

Tell me about a time when...

I once interviewed a candidate for a customer facing role in a large organization.

Not only would the candidate need to meet with potential clients, they would need to travel with their teams, work in an open space environment, and communicate effectively with various levels and departments within the organization.

Unfortunately, the candidate had two major roadblocks:

> **ONE:** It was clear that they were unhappy in their current role, and they allowed that negativity to seep into their interview.
>
> They spoke badly about managers, about the overall operations, and worst of all, made it clear that they were leaving on bad terms.
>
> **TWO:** They did not make the effort to present themselves as a professional that could walk into the role and gain credibility and likeability.
>
> They came in wearing ill fitted and wrinkled clothing, and their hygiene was questionable. It was clear they did not take the time to put themselves together in a way that said, "I belong in front of your customers."

The moral of the story is that no matter what struggles you are facing in your current role, or in the inability to find a role, leave that all at the door.

When you walk into an interview, remember that the interviewer doesn't know how great your personality is yet, or how hard you work; give them the opportunity to get to that stage.

4   THE COMPANY YOU KEEP

Remember your mom telling you not to hang out with the bad kids in school? If she could have continued to nag you through university, your first job and beyond, you would have been better off for it. When you surround yourself with people who are positive, confident, respectful and lift you up, that's the only direction for you to head.

5   NETWORK. NETWORK. NETWORK.

When people say, "it's who you know," it is! You don't have to be best friends with the hiring manager, but being able to say "I met you at a networking event last week", or "I know a member of your team from an event we both attended", gives you an advantage over the other applicants.

When you walk into an interview having already made a connection with the person in front of you or a member of the team, it is an automatic ice breaker. You are also giving the company an internal reference, as someone they can speak to before the end of the recruitment process.

Lastly, most companies have internal referral programs where the employee will get paid to refer good people - you want to be that good person!

6   BE KIND

Not because you have to be to get the job, but because it's the right thing to do. Spend some time volunteering, mentoring and teaching. Selfishly, it's a great way to build up your resume, network and keep yourself busy; but even more, it feels darn good!

7   BE REALISTIC

It drives recruiters and hiring managers crazy when applicants apply for roles that are completely out of their level of expertise. There's a reason why postings ask for 5+ years of experience; a new grad isn't going to match that. It's your job to make sure you are realistic with the roles that you are applying for and not aim so high that your resume just lands in the garbage. Conversely, it's equally important that you recognize when you don't fit in with the required skills, and opt out of the application process yourself.

8   BE SELF-AWARE

Understand how you are representing yourself to your potential employers. Request recommendations on LinkedIn, clean up your Facebook and make sure your online and social media presence is "hire-worthy".

9   GO FOR IT

Don't second-guess whether to reach out to someone for help, to send an application or to take a chance on applying for a job that seems just too good to be true. Great jobs, and great people are out there, and someone is going to land them. Why can't it be you?

10   KEEP READING

The next few pages are going to help you through the next phases of your job hunt. Keep reading to learn about what to expect as the process continues so you feel prepared for each step, well before it arrives.

PERSPECTIVE

SO MANY PEOPLE AROUND THE WORLD WOULD GIVE ANYTHING FOR "MONDAY" TO BE THEIR BIGGEST WORRY.

NATASHA JESHANI

THE RESUME
PART 1

Take the time to understand the value of having a well thought-out and written resume. It doesn't have to be full of flash and flare but keep this top ten list in mind the next time you're updating your resume.

1   MARKET YOURSELF

Use your resume as a chance to market yourself. This is most likely your only way of making it into the company's radar and landing an interview, so spend time selling yourself.

2   SEARCHABILITY

Chances are, if you have a strong resume that clearly articulates your KSA's (knowledge, skills and abilities), you are going to be found online. Make it easy for recruiters to search for you on LinkedIn, resume databases, etc.

Here are some tips on how to generate relevant KSA's:

- Read the job posting and website carefully
- Be specific and to the point
- Provide examples to allow the reader to relate your experience to their own needs
- If you are going to use acronyms (like KSA), be sure to break it down
- Simple language works best - don't try to impress with big words and fancy sentence structure
- Don't copy and paste from the posting; use your own words

TIP: Don't underestimate the power of the searchable keywords. Think about the words that recruiters and hiring managers are typing into various social media and resume banks to try to find their right candidate. Ensure that you aren't being overly creative with your words, but instead, filling your page with words that would likely be used to find you.

For example, an executive assistant that wants to be found would have words like:

EXECUTIVE ASSISTANT | ADMINISTRATION | CUSTOMER SERVICE | SUPPORT

Instead of:

RIGHT HAND GURU | TYPER PRO | AWESOME GATEKEEPER

3 TWO HEADS ARE BETTER THAN ONE

Have someone else read your resume. If you don't have an HR or Recruiter friend, try someone that has some experience reading resumes and knows what a hiring manager would be looking for. At the very least, have someone edit your resume and cover letter for basic grammar and spelling.

4 USE OTHER RESOURCES

You don't have to look for a job alone; network, speak with recruitment agencies and go onto school alum boards. Use the help that's available out there to enhance your resume and strengthen your chances of getting it into the right hands.

5 DON'T BE SHADY

Recruiters see resumes all the time that leave out important details such as company names, how long you worked at a company, and when you graduated. This is all basic information that belongs on a resume so if you leave that off, they will be quick to wonder why that is.

I once began reviewing a candidate resume that lined up so well with my posting.

They took the time to review the posting, read up on what we did and what our products did, and crafted a strong resume.

I then moved on to LinkedIn to do my review there. Immediately, I realized that I was looking at two different messages. After ensuring I was reviewing the right candidate, it became clear that there was little in the resume that was accurate.

Dates were changed, titles were inflated, and the worst part was that neither of those real facts (shorter time lines or less glamourous titles) would have affected their ability to move forward in the process.

The moral of the story is to be confident in what you bring to the table and present your truth with honor. A decent recruiter will notice the holes in your story and a good recruiter will hold you to those lies.

 DON'T BE VAGUE

Be clear and concise in describing who you are and what you do. Keeping it vague makes it harder for recruiters to find out who you are and connect you to an open position.

DO THE WORK

Don't leave it up to an agency or a job board or the company to do the work that you could do. You need to ensure that you are updating your resume regularly, adding in the right information and tailoring it specifically to each company and position.

8 TAILORING

This applies to every single application. Take an extra few minutes to update the resume to what that position is looking for. Explain how you came to find their company and how you align with their goals. Each company and job is different, and your resume should reflect that.

9 BE REALISTIC

Don't stretch your resume farther than it can go. If you aren't qualified for a position, don't fill your resume with jargon or waste your time or the recruiter's time by being unrealistic with your applications.

No matter how you write it, if they want 5-7 years, you can't stretch out a 1-year co-op to make a match.

10 ALWAYS HAVE IT READY

Resumes should never be written from scratch when you are out of work and desperate for a job. Every time you get a job, take some time to update your resume and enhance the skills portion by including real time statistics. It's easy to write down what you do every day in the present; it gets much harder to remember the details once you've stepped away from the role.

MANAGERS

THEY DON'T WANT
TO HEAR ABOUT
WHAT YOU PLAN TO
DO IN THE **FUTURE**
THEY WANT TO SEE
WHAT YOU ARE DOING
TO MAKE A **POSITIVE**
IMPACT IN THEIR
ORGANIZATION **NOW**.

PAULINE O'MALLEY

THE RESUME
PART 2

Now that you have a general sense of what the resume is all about, let's get technical.

1   Do not include your picture, date of birth, gender or religion – not only do hiring managers not want to know this information, but in Canada, according to the Employment Standard Act, it's illegal for them to take this information into consideration. Don't make their lives harder, just remove it from your resume.

> The **Canadian Human Rights Act** and the **Employment Equity Act**, ensures equal opportunity to individuals who may be victims of discriminatory practices based on a set of prohibited grounds such as sex, sexual orientation, race, marital status, gender identity or expression, creed, age, colour, disability, political or religious belief.
>
> http://laws-lois.justice.gc.ca/PDF/H-6.pdf S.C. 1976-77, c. 33, s. 1; current citation: R.S.C. 1985, c. H-6.

2   Don't put sentences like "met targets" or "exceeded goals" without explaining what those goals and targets were. Without the numbers to support your accomplishments, those statements have no meaning to the hiring manager.

3   If you did something that really made an impact, underline or **bold** the statement to make it stand out and catch the reader's attention.

4   If you include an objective, make it relevant to the position, and not the typical "I want to move into a role where I will be challenged."

5   Start at the most recent points and work your way back. There are general guidelines in resume writing – follow them.

6   Don't get too fancy with logos and formats – not all computers are compatible with all documents and templates.

7   Keep the font simple. Yes, Times New Roman can get boring, but it's legible. The fancier you get, the harder it is for the reader to skim. The more you slow them down, the faster they will toss your resume aside.

8   Size matters. Shrinking the font to 8 points to squeeze your content into 2 pages doesn't count. It's irritating to the reader (especially the ones that read print copies) and doesn't hide the fact that you weren't able to condense your content.

9   A resume with more than 2 colors (black and maybe blue for links) is just going to distract the reader and detract from the quality of your resume. Getting creative with resumes has a time and a place, but generally speaking, most applications will do well without it.

10 Line up your dates. Most recruiters are trained to skim through to make sure there are no gaps in your resume and that the dates line up. Make it easy to see that they do and if they don't, make sure you have included a good reason why.

BONUS BULLET:

11 Be aware of your own industry standards. A good idea is to focus on tailoring your resume differently for different roles. For example, the skills you choose to highlight for an administrative role will be different from a resume tailored to a digital marketing position.

"

ALL
EXPERTS
WERE
ONCE
BEGINNERS.

ANONYMOUS

THE COVER LETTER

1 NEW INFORMATION

A cover letter gives you a chance to tell a story about who you are and why you're right for the job. Don't waste it by adding the same information that they are going to find on your resume.

2 MENTION YOUR REFERRAL

Are you being referred by someone internally? Make sure to mention it right away and give yourself the added benefit of a few extra minutes of their attention. Generally, companies will follow up with the person that has referred a candidate to provide feedback. Even if you don't make the cut, you could end up getting some valuable inside information into why.

3 ADDRESS IT TO THE RIGHT PERSON

With LinkedIn and websites, you can generally figure out who you need to address your cover letter to. You can even give the company a quick call and ask them who to make your cover letter out to. At the very least, use HR or Recruitment Team. Put in the effort to avoid having to write "To whom it may concern".

4 TAGLINES

If you think about the major corporate brands out there, you can probably remember their slogan or tagline. Almost every company has one. Go onto their site or read the preamble on the job posting. Then, figure out how you align with that tagline and tell them.

5   CONNECT ON A DEEPER LEVEL

Live in the community? Did a co-op with the company? Worked for a competitor? Find a way to connect the dots.

6   DO THE RESEARCH

Get on their website and start to read up on their corporate culture, philanthropic work and mission statements. Use this to explain why you would fit right in.

7   ONE PAGE

It should not take more than one page for you to connect with the hiring manager. In fact, exceeding this general expectation sends the wrong message about your communication skills.

What message you ask? Wordiness and the inability to be succinct.

Put another way, if you require 2-3 pages to share your introduction with the hiring manager, your burden of truly amazing goes up significantly. It is a true skill to be able to understand the purpose of a document (such as a cover letter) and be able to introduce your story in a way that draws the reader in and leaves them wanting to know more.

If everything you have ever accomplished is in the cover letter, it likely won't get read through. If it does, it will reduce the need for the hiring manager to bring you in to meet with you.

8   MATCH YOUR RESUME LAYOUT

Do your best to match font and size to make it look seamless as the recruiter or hiring manager reviews your resume.

9   PDF AS ONE DOCUMENT

Whenever possible, make the cover letter and resume into one PDF document. This makes it easy for the reader to print one document and have everything together. This works best when emailing in your application and attaching a file.

10   CONTACT INFORMATION

Sign off with your contact information and indicate your preferred method of communication.

I once had a candidate submit a resume through a client's online portal. This was a very basic portal that simply requested you to upload your resume and cover letter; no fill in the blanks, no sign-up required.

After a quick glance, I was ready to hop on a quick call with the candidate to ask a few follow up questions.

The problem? There was no phone number provided.

Recruiters are resourceful, so I decided to email them.

Can you guess what happened next? There was no email provided!

The candidate had forgotten to provide their basic contact information.

If I didn't have a significant number of applicants, I could have done a little digging online and found it, but this candidate added work that I didn't need to do because I had 20 other candidates who were much easier to access, with similar resumes.

The moral of the story is to triple check that the basics are included.

One best practice is to get a couple of your colleagues to review your resume before you start submitting it. A professional doesn't have to redo your resume, they can also be your editor and second set of eyes.

"

BECASUE
YOU'RE AMAZING,
JUST THE WAY
YOU ARE.

BRUNO MARS

SOCIAL MEDIA

Now that social media is in common use, your resume isn't the only thing that is representing you. Google, Facebook, LinkedIn and Twitter are the most common platforms for an employer to do their online digging. It's up to you to make sure that you are being represented the right way on these sites.

1   LINKEDIN FACTS

Make sure that the companies, dates, titles and descriptions on LinkedIn and your resume match – and make sure they are the truth. HR and Recruitment can be a small world and it's easy to find out when things aren't aligning the way they should. Use LinkedIn to showcase your work and highlight your strengths. It's essentially an online version of your resume.

2   WHO YOU ARE CONNECTED TO MATTERS

Make sure you are connected to old co-workers, bosses and people from your past to show that you can make and maintain relationships. It also demonstrates that you aren't constantly burning bridges.

3   USE PROFESSIONAL PICTURES

Regardless of where you post, profile pictures will generally come up on a Google search, so be sure to have a professional picture up – especially on LinkedIn.

4   GOOGLE YOURSELF

Take a moment to dig into your own world and see what comes up. Make sure that there is nothing you wouldn't want to represent you popping up. Also take the time to enhance your security settings to block things like personal sites from employers.

*turn to **page 102** for a quick checklist of things to look for when focusing on your social security settings.

5   CONTROVERSY VS. DISRESPECT

It's okay to not agree with people on social media and to express your opinion but be careful how you express your differences. Once you insult or disrespect other people, you burn that bridge and potentially others who can see your posts.

6   DON'T SPEAK BADLY ABOUT ANY PAST EMPLOYER OR CO-WORKER

This one feels like it should go without saying, and yet this happens far too often. It may be as simple as a company asking a question over LinkedIn and people commenting with their negative experiences, potentially forgetting that others are able to view their comments. An easy check is to ask yourself "how would I feel if my boss, friend or family read this post?"

7   PLAGIARISM

Remember in school, when you had to cite your sources? Social media is a great tool for taking other people's ideas and building upon it, but respect that it was someone else's idea and give them credit.

Using another person's picture for a post you're going to make? Tag them in it – it's not only the right thing to do, it gives them some added exposure and will likely garner a like or a retweet. Building your brand on the backs of others will never win you points in the long run.

8 HONESTY

Getting caught lying about being sick is one of the most common ways that social media can catch you in a lie. There are also things like being on disability or going on job interviews. If you are putting it out there on social media, assume your boss is seeing it. Nothing is truly private.

If you are active on any social media site, be aware of what you are saying.

There was once a TV talk show group on Facebook and the topic was "calling in sick when you aren't truly sick".

It generated some fun conversations and for the most part, people were respectful and just trying to be funny.

One person decided that they were going to comment with "should be at work right now, but the beach was calling my name #wealldoit"

The hashtag garnered more comments and likes and got the comment some attention.

The replies ranged from disappointment at cheating the system, to "props".

Then, everyone saw this comment:

"Hi [insert employee name here]. I'm happy to see that you enjoy [insert talk show name here] too, looks like we share the same taste in TV talk shows.

Not so happy to see that you skipped out on your meetings, left your coworkers to pick up the slack and put in writing that you were sick, when clearly this is not the case.

Please give me a call when you get home from the beach."

The moral of the story is to assume that everything you write will be read by your parents, your partner, your children, your clients, co-workers and even your boss!

"

YOU GET IN

LIFE

WHAT YOU HAVE

THE **COURAGE** TO

ASK FOR.

OPRAH WINFREY

NETWORKING

Networking is often seeing as a tough thing to do successfully. I want to share a few ways to network that aren't so challenging and can still yield some great results.

1 ATTEND A WORKSHOP

This is an easy way to meet likeminded individuals without the awkwardness of having to necessarily exchange cards and talk shop, unless you want to.

2 BE OPEN TO TELLING YOUR STORY

At a coffee shop and sitting next to someone friendly? Don't shy away from building up a conversation and sharing your story. It's great practice, and you never know who they are and how they may be able to connect you to someone in the future.

3 HAVE A NETWORK BUDDY

It's always easier to walk into a room and see a familiar face. If this is you, ask a friend or colleague to join you to give you the confidence boost you need.

4 ONLINE NETWORKS

Social media provides a great opportunity to engage with networks without ever leaving home or work. Take advantage of engaging with the right people, sharing posts and articles and building up an online professional network.

5 WEBINARS

Just because you can't see who else is attending a session, doesn't mean that you can't make a connection. There is the speaker, the chat, and the organizer that are guaranteed to interact with you to some degree.

6 MENTOR / MENTEE

If you struggle in group settings, be open to creating a mentor/mentee relationship and develop 1 connection at a time.

"

REACHING
YOUR GOAL
IS AN OBVIOUS
WIN.
IN ORDER TO
LEARN FROM
YOUR JOURNEY,
YOU MUST BE
MINDFUL
AND PRESENT.

NATASHA JESHANI

THE PHONE SCREEN

Every hiring manager is different and will have their own ways of doing things. Some may pre-arrange the call, while others will catch you off guard. Here are a few quick tips on what to be prepared for the moment you've sent in your application.

1   KNOW YOUR STORY

Be able to succinctly answer the "tell me about yourself" question and keep it focused on the professional side of your world.

2   KNOW YOUR CURRENT ROLE (OR MOST RECENT ROLE) WELL

Be prepared to answer situational questions around what you were responsible for, who you reported to, the size of the team and overall organization, and how you made an impact.

3   NOTICE

Know how much notice you need to give and if successful, when you can start.

4   SALARY EXPECTATIONS

While it's no ones business how much you currently make, or what you made in your last role, it's only fair that they know your expectations for this opportunity. Be able to come up with a realistic range that you would genuinely accept at.

5   KNOW WHERE YOU'VE APPLIED TO

Be able to speak to the company that you applied to. Simple information like their line of work and location are a great start.

6   KNOW WHAT YOU'VE APPLIED TO

Know the title of the job and the basic requirements.

7   DON'T GET SCHOOLED

Be sure you know the dates of your courses, degrees, etc. and be able to speak to why you chose to take that education, what you gained from it, and how you apply it to your current role.

8   CONTACT

When you first get a call, it's doesn't always come with advanced notice, which means that you may not catch their name. At the end of the call, make sure to reconfirm their name, title and contact info in case you want to follow up.

"

DO THE BEST
YOU CAN
UNTIL YOU
KNOW BETTER
THEN, WHEN YOU
KNOW BETTER,
DO BETTER.

MAYA ANGELOU

THE
INTERVIEW

Congratulations! You've reached the interview stage. Let's take a moment to focus on the fact that you've made it this far, and the hard work that went into getting here.

Far too often we dismiss this step if we don't get the job. Getting in front of a hiring manager is no small feat and is something to be proud of.

The next section will focus on ensuring that you are well equipped to walk into the interview confident, professional and with the right tools to be successful.

1   BE POSITIVE

It is hard to resist a candidate that walks in with a positive attitude, an upbeat personality and an optimistic outlook on their career.

2   KNOW WHAT YOU WANT

The company has a clear set of goals and objectives. Make sure you can demonstrate that you have the same for yourself. Understand where you want to be in 1, 3 and 5 years and work that into your answers.

3   WIFM

"What's in it for me?" (or WIFM) is a term that has been around for a long time. Remember that the interview is about what's in it for them (in hiring you). Take the time to explain to them what the benefits of hiring you are and what your deliverables will be.

4   YOU NEED TO BE READY TO ASK QUESTIONS TOO

Here are 5 great questions to ask when you're in the interview:

1. What do you expect of me in the first 3 months of coming on board?
   > Show them that you are ready to work

2. How would you describe the main strengths of your top performers?
   > Show them you want to align with the best

3. What drives results for your team/company?
   > Show them that you are invested in them

4. What activities do employees do together outside of work?
   > Show them you are a team player and want to fit in

5. What is the biggest challenge that the team/company faces today and how can my role impact that change positively?
   > Show them you plan to make a difference

5   STAY FOCUSED

It's easy to go off on a tangent or let a conversation with the interviewer take you away from your main goal. Stay focused on the issue at hand – getting that job! You want the focus of the interview to be on you and why you are the best person for the job, but also about the interviewer and what they have to say.

DON'T GET DISCOURAGED

Interviews are nerve-racking for everyone, even the interviewers. Don't let a tough line of questioning rattle you. If you can't think of an answer, take a deep breath, think about the answer and then deliver. Don't rush to say the first thing that pops into your mind to get the question over with – chances are the next question isn't going to be much easier.

 EXPRESS YOUR DESIRE TO LAND THE JOB

Don't be afraid to tell them exactly why you want the job.

Here are a few great ways to show them you're sold:

1. Tell them how excited you are to feel so aligned to their needs.

2. Provide examples of how you've done similar work and express your interest in continuing to use that value-add skill set with their company.

3. When you hear something that makes you confirm your interest in the company or role, say so.

4. When you are saying goodbye, don't be afraid to be vulnerable and say "thank you for taking the time to meet with me. This interview has reaffirmed my interest in the role and the company, and I would love to be considered for the role and to move on to the next steps."

8 REMEMBER YOUR INTERVIEW STARTS
IN THE PARKING LOT

Anyone you meet from the time you park until the time you sit in that room could have an impact on the success of your interview, so be on point from the start. Hold the door open for someone coming in, smile at people in the hallways, greet the receptionist with respect and take the time to speak to them.

9 HAVE FUN

Interviews can be a lot of fun if you put in the effort to make it that way. Make a joke (when it's appropriate), smile and don't be afraid to bond with people. This is going to make a big impact on your life, but it doesn't have to be a miserable experience.

DON'T FOCUS ON THE DOLLARS

Everyone in that room understands that the dollars are important. A good HR or recruiting manager will have already asked for a salary range from you during the phone screening or application process. This may feel early for you, but they want to make sure they aren't wasting their time interviewing a 100k candidate for a 50k job.

Regardless of whether money has been discussed, use this time to sell yourself, not to start negotiations.

11 DO YOU KNOW WHAT TO EXPECT NEXT?

Ask them. The worst feeling in the world is to walk out of an interview feeling like you have no idea how it went, no idea what's coming next or what to do. This feeling is so easily avoidable.

Find out if you have answered all their questions; make sure you ask if it's okay to connect if you think of anything else. Find out what the hiring process is and what the next steps are.

Then thank them for their time and walk out with your head high!

PAUSE

THINK OF
SOMETHING
YOU CAN DO
TODAY THAT YOU
COULDN'T
DO THIS TIME
LAST YEAR.

NATASHA JESHANI

THE INTERVIEWER

Here is a list of ten things you should know about the person that is interviewing you.

1   THEY WANT TO HIRE YOU

Remember that they want you to be the right person for the job, so they can fill the position. Whether the person is in HR, a Recruiter or a Hiring Manager, they all have the same goal – to fill that job opening.

The interviewer is walking into that interview hoping that you are going to be the next employee – it's up to you to convince them that that is you.

So, stay positive and walk in confidently - they are on your side.

2   THEY DON'T HAVE A LOT OF TIME

You aren't the only one being interviewed. Every candidate has had their resume read, been phone screened and had an interview scheduled, most likely all by that same person now sitting in front of you.

They don't have the time to respond to the several follow up emails and calls you send to keep checking to see if you've got the job.

They know you'd love an answer right away and chances are, they would love to give one. BUT…they have a lot of steps on the back end before they can do that.

So be patient and give them some extra time to get back to you.

3 THEY MAY NOT BE THE DECISION MAKER

Often, the person sitting in front of you during an interview isn't the one making the final decision (or at the very least, not the only member). They need to get budgets approved, confer with others who will be dealing with your position and must adhere to hiring rules and timelines.

So, do your best to find out what all the above obstacles are so you can do your best to assist them (or at the very least, not make their jobs harder).

4 THE COST OF A BAD HIRE IS MORE THAN YOU MIGHT THINK

The person interviewing you has a lot at stake when they make the final "you're hired" call. It's a lot more work for them to hire the wrong fit and need to get rid of them, then to really take their time with hiring.

There's a common saying in the hiring world "slow to hire, quick to fire." It's an ideal that not many can follow.

So, explain to the interviewer why you are going to be a long-term fit and not a costly mistake.

5 THEY WANT TO LIKE YOU FOR YOU, NOT JUST FOR YOUR RESUME

Even if you have all the right skills and can do the job with your eyes closed, that doesn't mean that the job is necessarily yours. The person interviewing you has the added fortune of being able to hire someone that they like and want to deal with.

So, do your best to get along with the interviewer person-to-person, not just as potential future employer to potential future employee.

6 THEY NEED TO KNOW HOW YOU'LL WORK OUT WITH MANAGEMENT

Let's call it like it is, not everyone is fun to manage. You are being interviewed for a job and will have a boss. They need to figure out how you are going to be with that boss and whether you will get along.

So, demonstrate your ability to work well with others, express your opinions respectfully and effectively and be the type of employee that plays fair.

7 THEY WANT YOU TO DO SOME OF THE WORK TOO

Interviewers hate to do all the taking in the interview. The less you talk, the more work they must put in to make it through the interview.

So, work at providing succinct but accurate responses and give them what they want. If you know they are looking for an example of your strengths, make sure to add that in so they don't have to ask.

8 INTERVIEWER CUES AREN'T ALWAYS ACCURATE CUES

A good interviewer is trained not to show their full deck of cards. They might look stern and straight-faced, or nod fervently every time you answer a question. Don't take these as signs of how the interview is going and change direction.

Regardless of how the interview feels like it's going, it's your job to stay on point, on the ball and fight until the end.

9 THEY HAVE A JOB TO DO TOO

Like it or not, the person sitting in front of you is being judged on the outcome of that interview too. If you don't give them enough reasons to hire you, they can't.

So, be sure to remember that they have a boss, goals and expectations too. Learn more about them so you can help make them look good by hiring you.

10 THEY PUT IN THE TIME TO BE PREPARED AND EXPECT THE SAME IN RETURN

It takes a long time for an interviewer to prepare for an interview. They need to really learn who you are, research you on social media, have targeted and specific questions prepared, be equipped to take notes and remember as much as they can about the interview.

So, help them out by bringing your resume and the job posting, know the job description inside out, know what the company does, and be ready for the obvious questions that you know are coming.

"

THE
PERFECT JOB
MIGHT NOT EXIST
BUT **YOUR RIGHT**
TO CREATE ONE,
DOES.

NATASHA JESHANI

AFTER THE INTERVIEW

We now understand that it's important to ask your questions during the interview and to limit the amount of follow up with the hiring manager. Now, what questions do you ask to make sure you aren't leaving anything out?

1 CLARIFY ANY UNCERTAINTIES

Was there a question that threw you off, but you didn't get a chance to get clarification on? Do that before you leave.

2 COULD YOU GIVE ME SOME BRIEF INSIGHT INTO THE DAY-TO-DAY ROLE?

It's important to be able to understand the day-to-day role that you can't always get from a job posting, so don't be afraid to ask.

3 WHAT ARE YOUR TRAINING AND DEVELOPMENT OPPORTUNITIES?

You want to ensure that you can learn and grow. Ask about how they assist with that in a way that gets your question answered and shows your expectations.

4 WHAT ATTRIBUTES ARE YOU LOOKING FOR SOMEONE TO HAVE TO SUCCEED IN THIS ROLE?

Find out exactly what they are looking for and then show them how that's you.

5

WHAT SKILL SET GAPS DO YOU SEE IN THE TEAM THAT YOU WOULD LIKE TO FILL?

Again, learn where their weak points are and then show them your strengths in those areas.

6

WHAT ARE THE OPPORTUNITIES FOR ADVANCEMENT?

Be sure to express your desire to stay long term and inquire about what you would hope to get in return.

7

WHAT IS YOUR FAVOURITE THING ABOUT WORKING AT THE COMPANY?

Give them a chance to sell the company to you and build a little rapport along the way.

8

WHAT ARE THE NEXT STEPS IN THE HIRING PROCESS?

Be sure to understand what is expected next and how you can provide them with as much of that upfront as possible.

9

CAN I PROVIDE YOU WITH ANY ADDITIONAL INFORMATION SUCH AS REFERENCES, THAT WOULD BE HELPFUL?

Don't wait for them to ask. If they say they will email you if they need your references, leave it. If they say, 'yes, please provide us with your references', have them ready to hand over immediately.

10 BE AWARE OF THE TIME

If you were scheduled for a one-hour interview and the interview is running long, ask for permission to follow up with some questions and acknowledge the time. If they don't mind going over, then continue with your questions. Show them that you respect their time and have strong time management skills.

"

AT THE END OF THE DAY,
IT'S NOT ABOUT
WHAT YOU HAVE OR
EVEN WHAT YOU'VE
ACCOMPLISHED.
IT'S ABOUT WHO
YOU'VE **LIFTED UP**,
WHO YOU'VE **MADE BETTER**.
IT'S ABOUT WHAT
YOU'VE **GIVEN BACK**.

DENZEL WASHINGTON

THE OFFER

This why you picked up the book. You put in the hard work and prepared for this moment right here.

Just because you got the offer, does not mean you have the job. This may be the most important part of the process, because this is where you have an opportunity to control the outcome.

Far too often, this is the stage where candidates push too hard, act without thinking or make rash decisions.

Let's look at some important points to follow.

1   DON'T OVER NEGOTIATE

If a company offers you a fair compensation, it's ok to just take it. Not every employment relationship needs to begin with a push.

2   DON'T NEGOTIATE IF THEY SAY THIS IS THEIR BEST OFFER

Some companies have a policy whereby they present their best offer the first time around, no negotiating. If this has been made clear at the beginning of the offer process, it's important that you come back at them with a yes or no.

While companies should not hold it against you if you feel the offer is unfair and want to have a conversation about it, there are definitely some inflexible managers out there that are focused more on the process than the end result.

DON'T ACCEPT THE VERBAL OFFER

When a company calls and offers you a job, don't immediately say yes. Instead, thank them for the offer, let them know that you are happy to hear it and are looking forward to reviewing the offer in full.

READ THE OFFER LETTER AND CONTRACT

Not everything about the contract is going to be told to you over the phone. Make sure you understand what they are asking of you and what you are getting.

LOOK BEYOND THE SALARY

There is so much more to an offer than the salary. Remember to review vacation allotment, benefits, policies and practices to get the bigger picture.

REPLY BY THEIR DEADLINE

If you aren't sure you are going to accept, be sure to let the company know that you need more time. While this will likely not go over well and will give the immediate impression that you aren't as interested in them as they are in you, or that you have a potentially better offer coming, it is MUCH better than missing the deadline all together.

7 DON'T BE AFRAID TO ASK QUESTIONS

Even though you may not be comfortable negotiating your contract, that does not mean that you cannot seek clarification. Often contracts are worded in ways that are not overly simplified and asking a few clarifying questions can make a big impact on your decision.

8 BE GRACIOUS NO MATTER WHAT

If you are offered a job at a salary that isn't going to work, or you are no longer interested in the company, make sure that your no is polite and respectful. Just because they are a no right now, does not mean that they will always be a no in the future.

Keep in mind also that people move companies and the manager from that company could easily be the manager of the next company you apply to down the road.

"

PREPARE YOURSELF
NOW,
FOR WHERE YOU
WANT TO BE IN
5 YEARS.

SALIM JANMOHAMED

THE
CHECK
IN

Have you ever taken a step back and re-evaluated the impression that you are making on hiring managers?

Here are a few "food for thoughts" on what you need to keep in check.

1 WORD WIZARD

There's a difference between using a robust vocabulary to show your grasp of the English language, and then there is "synonym-ing" your resume to death.

Sometimes, simple language goes a long way and doesn't make it look like you are trying too hard.

2 BE POSITIVE

Are you a Debby Downer? A Negative Nelly? That isn't fun for anyone, least of all someone that's able to hire you. It's okay to want to learn about the company and the position, but be careful not to look like you are finding reasons not to take the job.

3 PUSHING IS FOR DOORS

There is a limit to how much follow up, persistence and communication people can handle. Be sure to limit your communication to times when it's appropriate or requested and don't get so aggressive that you push yourself right out of the running.

4 WHAT YOU DID ON SATURDAY NIGHT ISN'T FOR ALL

As we discussed, your social media presence has an impact on how you are viewed, so don't display your less than picture perfect nights out for all to see, hear and read.

5 PAY ATTENTION

This starts with the resume and ends at the offer. Pay attention to things like the name of the person that is interviewing you, the company name and the title of the position. When you make mistakes that reveal your lack of knowledge of these basic details, you insinuate that you don't care.

6 R.E.S.P.E.C.T.

Even if you end up bonding over the phone screen and getting along great in the interview, don't lose your professionalism. Respect the job of the interviewer and their time, and don't set out to make a new friend or cross the line. Get to know the receptionist, but don't get her number and plan a fun night out.

7 DON'T ASSUME. IT MAKES AN ...

In the job search world, assuming can be a very dangerous thing. During the resume writing phase, don't assume the person reading your resume knows who you are and what you do; take the time to explain it. In the interview, don't assume the job is yours (or that you've bombed); stay even-keeled and consistent. During salary negotiations, don't assume your ask is too low or too high; try to find out their range.

8 I'M LITERALLY DYING - GETTING A JOB IS SO HARD!

No, you're not dying and no, it's not that hard. Don't overdo applications, resumes and interview responses. Be real, be you and be honest. When you start to exaggerate, it all starts to unravel.

9 TMI

There is such a thing as giving too much information. Whether it's going on and on in a 6-page resume or complaining for 10 minutes about your last manager when asked why you left your last company, don't give them more than they need to know. It's important to give all the important information, but not all the information.

10 WANT IT

It's a terrible feeling when you've got a candidate that looks great on paper and says all the right things, but clearly doesn't care if they get the job.

Show then that you want it from the very beginning. Make people feel wanted, cared about and important – it's human nature, why not use it your advantage?

BONUS BULLET:

11 WIFM: WHAT'S IN IT FOR ME?

Aside from the paycheck, a job should provide you with a sense of adding value, of growth and of enjoyment. Assess this in the first 3 months of your role and be sure to communicate both your positive experiences and areas of concern.

"

GO THROUGH THE
SMALL PAINS **NOW**,
TO AVOID THE
BIG PAINS **LATER**.

PROBLEMS DON'T
AGE WELL.

SALIM JANMOHAMED

THE JOB

You've landed your dream job – congratulations! This was no small feat and is something to be celebrated. BUT…now that your bum is in the seat, let's make sure it stays there.

1 UNDERSTAND YOUR MANAGER'S POINT OF VIEW

This doesn't mean that you turn into a "yes man/yes woman." Instead, take the time to see what they find important. Is it maintaining the budget? Sales goals? Customer service? Find their hot button and focus on it when pitching everything from taking a vacation, to taking a training course, to taking on more responsibility. Make it about their bottom line, not yours.

2 ALWAYS CREATE CREDIBILITY

Bosses want to see that you are credible when you are pitching something to them. Create an environment where co-workers, other managers and even clients will speak to your strengths.

3 CONSISTENCY IS KEY

Be consistent in your work, in your words and most importantly, in who you are.

Here are a few good questions to ask yourself, to see if you are consistent:

1. Does my resume truly reflect the work that I do?
2. Will my references align with my resume?
3. Does my LinkedIn reflect my resume and my day-to-day roles and responsibilities?
4. Do I say what I mean in a genuine and authentic way?

5. Am I confident in the work that I do now, and in the work I want to do moving forward?
6. Am I setting myself up for success by surrounding myself with people that will help me achieve my goals?

4 BE RELIABLE

Common sense, you say? Then this should be an easy one to achieve. Show up to work on time, do the work that you're expected to do and be there when you're needed.

5 GO ABOVE AND BEYOND

Don't let the job take over your life or lose your sense of work-life balance. That said, ensure that if a project needs an extra few hours, you take the time to put that effort in. Everything is within reason but when you start, you'll need to make an investment into the role and the company.

6 RAISE YOUR HAND

Take advantage of opportunities to further your job growth.

Opportunity to train a new employee? Give it a try and see how much you learn (along with the brownie points).

Traveling to a customer site or trade show? Why not take advantage of the networking opportunity and get away from the office for a few days?

BE FLEXIBLE

Things change – new employees start, and old employees go. In other words, SH*T happens! Don't let it rattle you and throw you off your game. Learn to adapt to the changes quickly and spot the positives.

 BE PERSONABLE

You weren't just hired for what you could do, but also for how you could do it. It's important to take the time to speak with the others in the office, be friendly and approachable and have people want to work with you.

 SAY PLEASE

Take this one literally first. When asking for anything, do it politely. That being said, don't forget to ask for things that you want. It's okay to want to take a training course, take a few days off or for just a little extra help. Remember that the person on the other side expects respect and courtesy – whether it seems that way or not.

10 SAY THANK YOU

Did a co-worker get something to you quicker than usual? Did the boss give you some extra perks? Did someone bring in a cake for your birthday? Don't forget to remind people of how much you appreciate these things. It encourages people to want to do nice things for you again.

"

NEVER STOP **GROWING**.
WHEN YOU CONTINUE
TO GROW,
THE COMPANY THAT
YOU WORK FOR
GROWS
SO IT'S ACTUALLY
TWO FOLD.

JESSE MCNEIL

CLOSING

Finding, landing and keeping a job is not easy. Employment rates fluctuate constantly, economies change, technology advances, new generations are born, and people change. There are so many reasons to start fresh, build new careers and move on to bigger and better things.

Being prepared for these events is key.

If you go to this point in the book, you now have the tools you need to apply for jobs, network with the right industry professionals, go for job interviews, accept an offer and start a new job successfully.

Take the time to complete the questionnaires and worksheets and fill out the checklists.

Use these tools to build yourself up to be the best job seeker, interviewee and employee you can be!

Good luck (even though we both know luck has nothing to do with it!).

CHECKLISTS & RESOURCES

SOCIAL MEDIA SECURITY
SETTINGS CHECKLIST

Take a moment to review the following social media settings and strategies:

- [ ] You can control what information you fill out when you sign up – use your own discretion

- [ ] Create smart passwords for all accounts that include symbols, letters and numbers

- [ ] When password security questions are standard, you aren't required to be truthful. When the only available question is 'what is your mothers maiden name?', you can answer this however you wish

- [ ] Use private browsing when using public systems. This will ensure all cookies, browser history and temporary files are deleted

- [ ] All social media accounts allow you to control you level of transparency – visit your security settings on each platform

- [ ] Set a google alert and get notified anytime your name is mentioned online

LINKEDIN

- Hover over your profile picture in the upper right-hand corner and select the "Privacy and Settings" option from the drop-down menu

FACEBOOK

- Access that "Privacy Settings and Tools" panel to control your settings

TWITTER

- To make your Twitter account private, click the wheel icon in the top right of your homepage and select "Settings", then select "Security and Privacy". Under "Privacy," check the box "Protect my tweets"

INSTAGRAM

- To keep your photos private, select "Edit Your Profile" next to your profile picture and turn on the "Posts are Private" settings

INTERVIEW PREP CHECKLIST

THE BASICS
Company Name:
Location:
Interview Date:
Interview Time:
Interviewer Name:
Interviewer Title:

THE TO DO
☐ Print 2 copies of your resume

☐ Print the job description – read it thoroughly

☐ Print your 3 references – ideally someone you have worked for, someone you have worked with and someone that has worked for you

☐ Pick out a professional outfit, even if it is a casual environment

THE TO KNOW
☐ Review the website ahead of time and know what they do

☐ Know the role of the interviewer

☐ Have questions prepared for the end of the interview

☐ Ability to speak to the following:
  > Your previous job titles
  > Length of time you were with the company
  > Who you reported to
  > Description of your roles and responsibilities
  > Ability to speak to the quality of your work
  > Be prepared to answer the salary question
  > Be prepared to know how much notice you need to give and why

REMEMBER: Past performance is a strong indicator of future performance. Show your interviewer how you were an asset in previous roles, and how that will carry over to fulfilling their needs.

Know the answers to the following questions:

1. Why are you applying for this role?

2. What makes you the ideal candidate?

3. What skills do you bring to the position that make you a good fit?

4. Are there gaps in your resume or areas your interviewer is going to ask you to elaborate on? Be prepared to answer.

5. What specific projects or tasks were big wins for you, and why?

6. Think of things that make up who you are as a person outside of work.

INTERVIEW FOLLOW UP GUIDE

PART 1:
Thank your interviewer for their time with:
- a. A handwritten thank you note or

- b. A personalized thank you email

PART 2:
Follow up with any promised documentation such as references, written samples or test answers

PART 3:
Review the interview process and gauge for yourself
- a. What went well?

- b. What did not go well?

- c. Did you leave feeling like your questions had been answered?

- d. Did you remember to share everything you wanted to about yourself?

- e. Were there any red flags?

PART 4:
Follow up if the follow up period indicated in the interview has passed by via:
- a. Email or

- b. Phone Call

FIRST DAY CHECKLIST

- [ ] Planned outfit for the first day – ensuring it aligns with corporate culture and policies

- [ ] Pack your bag
  - > Lunch and a snack
  - > Notepad and pen
  - > Cash (just in case)
  - > Parking pass (if required)

- [ ] List of manager and co-worker names and an emergency contact in case something goes wrong

- [ ] Personal information for payroll – ensure you know what you're expected to bring ahead of time

- [ ] Job description – know what you're going to be doing on day 1

- [ ] Organizational chart – ask for one if they don't offer it

- [ ] Personal bio – everyone is going to want to know your story, have yours prepared

- [ ] Company bio – know as much about the company as you can
  - > Their products and services
  - > Their size
  - > Their team structures
  - > The various locations
  - > How you fit into the picture

- Get to work 10-15 minutes early
- Make sure you're wearing something that makes you feel confident and comfortable
- Charge your phone and don't forget to turn it onto silent once you get to the office
- Accept help as it's being offered
- Ask questions and be engaged in the onboarding process

QUESTIONNAIRE
WHY DO I WANT THIS JOB?

When you're looking for a new job, it's often difficult to get a sense of the role with just a job posting and a website.

Here are a few questions to ask yourself before or during the hiring process to see for yourself if the job is right for you:

1. Does the list of job duties get you excited?

2. Will the role allow you to grow in some way?

3. Will you learn a new skill? Or deepen your knowledge in an existing skill?

4. Are you going to be compensated fairly for the role you will be doing?

5. Does the salary align with your needs?

6. Will the manager support your career growth?

7. Will you be comfortable approaching your manager in times of need?

8. Is there any opportunity to grow, laterally or vertically?

9. Ideal location for a commute?

10. Accessible for transit or parking?

11. Do your goals and values align with the company's?

12. Do you fit in to the overall culture of the team?

13. Will you feel proud to put this company on your LinkedIn and hand out your business card?

The main point of this questionnaire is to see if you want the job, even before you get a sense of whether they want you.

Financial requirements make these decisions more difficult, but if possible, if you start to answer no to more than 1 or 2 of the above questions, take some more time to assess your potential fit. It's okay to know yourself and your worth and wait for a better opportunity.

DAILY AFFIRMATION

Do you believe in the power of positive thinking? Energy? The Law of Attraction? Mindfulness?

I believe that the most important part of this entire journey is one that is already within you; and that is the ability to say you can attain this goal, and truly believe it.

Here is a simple exercise for you to do each morning before you start your day. Sample answers are also provided.

I AM GOOD AT:
       staying organized and on top of my tasks
I AM GREAT AT:
       connecting with others
I DESERVE:
       to be happy in my career
I BELIEVE IN:
       myself
I CAN HELP:
       others achieve their career goals and dreams
I NEED TO REMIND MYSELF TO:
       be patient
MY GOAL FOR TODAY IS:
       to motivate my readers to start their journey
MY GOAL FOR THE END OF THE WEEK IS:
       to provide my readers with the right tools to enhance their current career situation
MY GOAL FOR THE END OF THE MONTH IS:
       to congratulate readers on taking the first steps forward
MY GOAL FOR THE NEXT 3 MONTHS IS:
       to welcome my readers to their new careers

Ready to continue the learning?

Reach out to us at hello@tafaconsultingcorp.com
or visit tafaconsultingcorp.com

Made in the USA
San Bernardino, CA
06 July 2018